DOWN
MEMORY
LANE

BRENDA COOPER

authorHOUSE®

AuthorHouse™
1663 Liberty Drive
Bloomington, IN 47403
www.authorhouse.com
Phone: 1-800-839-8640

Published by AuthorHouse 01/05/2015

ISBN: 978-1-4969-4811-3 (sc)
ISBN: 978-1-4969-4799-4 (e)

Library of Congress Control Number: 2014918746

Life's roads are never straight- and you can only prepare yourself so much for what is around the next corner.

Fight

How would I define "Fight"?
My Mom - She is a real fighter
It seems that no matter what is dealt to her
She could scrap up some more fight

It didn't matter what it was
Us as small children – arguing amongst ourselves
My dad gone away from home while travelling
My Mom always had fight

Cheering us on in our sporting events
To making sure we did our best in school
She was always there for us
And fighting for us

Even when her health started to fail
It didn't matter what the diagnoses was
Lung cancer to incurable bone cancer
Even with the pain – My Mom always has Fight

As My Mom has always said–
God only gives you the hand you can handle
Well I guess he figures we can handle a lot
Because now we need to join my Mom and the Fight

"Thank You"

Thank You for being there when I was little
Thank You for putting up with me as a teen
Thank You for your guidance and patience
Thank You for your advice, even if not followed
Thank You for your support, no matter if you agreed
Thank you for lending an ear and a shoulder to cry on
But most of all "Thank You" for You being You and Letting Me be Me

****

The water is sparkling in the sun
Do I think I should turn and run
Life can deal one a poor hand
But it's how you play it, that makes it stand

Love can go smooth or hurt like hell
Because I have tripped and fell
Now I need to pick myself up
Regain my thoughts and start again

Trying Your Best – Not Perfection

I was taught to try my best
Put myself to the test
Push myself to my limits
But always try my best

It may appear I strive for perfection
But all I am trying to do is make a selection
In travelling the roads of life
With the least bumps and turns

****

Far From Perfect

I have tried to do my best
No matter what I was doing
Always putting myself to the test
To push my limits

Maybe I was not right
To expect the same from everyone else
Pushing them to fight
Because they think I expect perfection

I would expect no more than I would do
From all others – just try your best
But it appears all others do not have a clue
That I am far from perfect

My Best Friend, My Lover, My Soul Mate

Someone you can talk to
Someone you can confide in
Someone you want beside you
Someone that will walk beside you no matter what
That's why I know you are My Best Friend

Someone you can love
Someone with a special touch
Someone you can be intimate with
Someone that makes you feel loved
That's why I know you are My Lover

Someone to grow with
Someone to spend the rest of my life with
Someone you share a special connection with
Someone who gives back as much love as you give them
That's why I know you are My Soul Mate

Tough Love

Oh how to define Tough Love
Having time outs when children are young
Grounding children as they grow
But the toughest love of all is dealing with teenagers

Not realizing what they put their parents through
Questioning their every reasons as to why
Why can't I do this, why can't I go here
Why do I have to listen to you

Trying to implement values and guidance
Keeping your cool when challenged
Implementing rules and having them followed
But the toughest love of all is releasing them from your hold

Letting them learn things the hard way
Giving them the space and control of their lives
But keeping in contact with them
So they know you love and care for them

Tough Love tears the heart into pieces
Brings tears to the eyes of everyone
But you as a parent are hoping
That some day they will understand

Letting Go

There are many things in life
That we have to let go
Relationships, children and feelings
But the hardest one of all
Is letting go as a loved one passes

You prepare yourself as much as possible
But you wonder – Are you ever prepared
It is selfish to ask them to stay
To watch them suffer as their health is failing

So there comes a time
When we have to let them know
That we will be OK
As we let them go

An End ... To A New Beginning

You go through life
Figuring everything will remain the same
From birth to toddler
To youth to adulthood

Then something big causes a change
The death of a loved one
The void that it creates
Makes you think that the hurt will never go away

But actually it is a hurt
That will eventually change into memories
The memories that you will always have
Of that special person you lost

Instead of looking at it as an end
It needs to be looked at as a beginning
A beginning of your life full of their love and memories
And a beginning of the continuance of your changed life.

You sit, you look, you listen
You feel, you touch, you hear
Day in and day out
Week in and week out

Everything seems the same
No matter the day of the week
We continue with our lives
Month by month and year by year

****

Life can deal hard hands to play
You think you have the right cards
Until you are dealt a wrong mix
No trump, no run and no face card

****

The water trickles down the stream
Like a tear down my cheek
When I think about how much you're hurting
It makes my heart ache

You may not believe me, when I say
I feel the hurt you are feeling
And I want to take it away
But I know I can't, even if I try

The moon is full and bright
The air is free and slight
The smell of the evening is sweet
And the lovers do meet

Hand in hand and lips to lips
The lovers heart beat flips
They whisper in each other's ear
I love you and they make it clear

****

The horses are seen across the field
As the morning mist is clearing
On their back legs, they start their day by rearing
Before they gallop down to the creek for their morning drink

Their ears are up listening for day break
As the sun peeks above the horizon
The sunlight heats up the air
And the morning sounds filter loud and clear

I will always be there when things are good
I will always be there when things are bad
I will always be there when things are sad
I will always be there

****

My love for you deepens each and every day
Because I know that you are here to stay
The distance we have between us is just miles
Because our hearts have joined as one

You are so trusting and gentle in your touch
And I can see that you care so very much
The look in your eyes gives it away
The look of love that melts my heart

I get so scared of the way I feel
My heart aches for you because my feelings are so real
I miss your hugs when you are away
But I know that you will return

****

I really love you with all of my heart
I opened up and let you in
Now I am hurting and feel like –
My heart is broken in two

I'm sure time will heal
What has been broken
And we can restart
The feelings we know are there

****

Life is what we make it and no more
Even though we think we know what is in store
We think things are set out for us
Until it changes and the road makes a turn

There is one thing I know and that is for sure
I want you in my life until death do us part
The good and the bad I want to be there for you
And I know that I will always be true

I have found my soul mate in you
You have captured my heart and soul
Which I never thought anyone would do
I know I have found the man I want to spend
the rest of my life with – in You

****

There is something between us
That I know I cannot explain
The pain that I am now feeling
Will disappear with time

I hope you know, how much I love you
And how I will always be there
To help you through troubled times
And to show you how much I care

****

I want you to know
How much I care
Because I have found
Someone that is so rare

You have such a gentle touch
And I know that you care very much
The love in your eyes says it all
The same love you say when you call

Even though there are miles between us
Our love grows in meets and bounds
My feelings for you grow stronger each day
And how I know you are in my life to stay

We have a lot of hurdles to overcome
But I know we will get through
And whatever else is dealt our way
Because of our trust and openness

The open communication lines make it easy
To talk to you about everything
I can give my heart and soul
And I know you will keep it close to yours

The Eyes of The Ocean

Your eyes are as blue as the ocean
They can be as gentle as the summer breeze
Or as rough as the crashing waves
But they will always be as blue as the ocean

The gentleness that you can show
Comes from deep inside the heart
It is shown in your touch
As well as deep within your eyes of the ocean

Your gentleness can turn as quickly as it starts
But I've always known that deep inside
Your heart – is the love and gentleness
You can share with the ones that surround you

You must always remember
That your pride may need to be set aside
And let the roaring waves in
Your eyes of the ocean – start to calm

Once you start to realize
What life has to offer
You can start fresh
And look deep inside of your eyes of the ocean

In reality he is a young man
But his maturity is well beyond his years
He enjoys life in general
With a sense of humour

Whether it be snow boarding for fun
Or fulfilling his duties in the army
He always has his wits about him
Which helps him with life decisions

Miles away from home
Doesn't seem to affect his being
Although he may miss his roots
He is still young enough with no responsibilities

A lot of life is ahead
With decisions of reality to be made
Near home or far, far away
He needs to be happy no matter what

****

Caring, compassion and love
Three words that I would not have used
To describe my Dad
Because I did not know

He had given his Mom
These three things
When she needed them most
Caring, compassion and love

I'm Sorry

You go through life thinking you are making the right decisions
Not only for yourself but for everyone involved
Some decisions you made you knew were right
But there are some that have really hurt the ones you love

Making life that much easier
In the end may not have been
The hurt that has been caused
May never go away

Taking things away
And giving things up
May not have been the right thing to do
Even though life has continued

The road has been bumpy
And the turns have been sharp
I thought I was making the right decisions
And I am Sorry if I have hurt you

The hurt I have caused will never go away
Too many lives affected
By the changes in life
That I had made

Again, I am sorry
For making your lives so difficult
Maybe when you grow up
You can be a better person than I have been

My Feelings For You

When you're young, life goes slow
As you grow, life becomes fast
As life becomes fast, it also becomes busy
Career, kids and home life – a lot to balance

You then entered into my life
Like the gentleman – you are
First date was comfortable
With no pressure attached

As we talked on the phone each night
We got to know each other well
You reached for my heart
And stole it along with my soul

Miles between us didn't seem to matter
My love for you continues to grow
At times my heart aches
And at times my heart bursts

You fill the void that was in my life
Along with love that I can give
To you and only you
As my heart is overwhelmed with that love

I am yours forever
That much I know
And I can hardly wait
For us to become one

Life is short – as we now know
You are my soul mate
Now and forever – as we walk hand in hand
Down the road of life

It seems as though, I am always unhappy
No matter what I do or say, it is not right
I try so hard to give what is needed
But it never seems to be enough

I am not happy with myself
And life seems so difficult
It appears that I am the one with the problem
And never seems to be able to solve it

Sometimes you wonder if......
Then you realize that if you did
Too many people would be hurt
But they would get over it

They say time heals the heart
And memories fill that void
So everyone would continue with life
As they are suppose to do

Why I Love You

You were a gentleman when we first met
That remains the same today
You make me face grey areas
You look out for my best interests

You give me the support I need
You tell me what I want to hear and what I don't
You are everything I need in a companion
Caring, trust and a helping hand

But most of all
The one thing
That keeps me going
Is your love for me

I see that love in your eyes
I feel that love in your touch
Every time our lips meet
That love deepens

Even though there is hurt
Attached to that love
The love is more powerful
And is overwhelming

I love you for all these reasons
And many more
But most of all it is
The love I know you have for me

Remember – Be Yourself

Going through life as a child can be easy
Going through life as a teen can be difficult
Peer pressure, stress of school
And maybe pressure from parents

All these things have an
Influence on your life
Whether it be good or
Whether it be bad

They are always considered
A learning experience
Learning from your mistakes
Making choices you live with

One thing through all of this
Is to remember not to
Lose yourself
And to be yourself

Love – Deep Down

Going through life
Finding what is important
To you
To no one else
But you

Life brings many
Trials and tribulations
Mistakes and learning experiences
Needing help
And asking for it

Life can be filled
With happiness
And sadness
But life is important
And people are important

The people you chose
To have involved in your life
You make those choices
Or don't make those choices
Along with those people

Comes relationships
Friendships and family
Attached with this circle of people
Comes unconditional love
Love that is from deep inside

A love that does not change
A love that wants to be shown
Not kept caged up inside
A love that needs to be expressed
A love that is never lost

Always remember
This love is for you
Expressed or not
It is always there
Deep down inside

Parents – Their Love

Two people become one
Sharing love, companionship and trust
From this children are born
Unconditional love is more meaningful

Through the eyes of the children
Parents can be cool
They can be difficult
But there is always unconditional love

Parents can be helpful
They can be hurtful
But through all these experiences
Unconditional love is present

Parents are always there
When you need them
And even when you don't
But the love is always flowing

The guidance, the trusting hand
The advise that is given
Whether taken or not
The love is always overwhelming

Parents are not around forever
That is surely learned
But one thing to remember
The love they have given is there

Brenda Cooper

The love never dies
It is a warm feeling
That came from their heart
Deep down inside

Even though your parents
May physically be gone
The love they left behind
Will always be there

Mothers

They carry you for nine months
They go through pain to give you birth
They have that loving touch
The bonding that never fades

They are there when you are hurt
They have that special touch
To take the pain away
And that loving kiss

Yes, that kiss that makes
Everything better
At least for the moment
All is good

Mothers are there for guidance
They are there for heartache
To pick up the pieces
And to reconfirm their love

They support you
They help you – even if you say "No"
They want you to realize
That they are always there for you

They feel what you feel
The hurt, the happiness
The disappointment
And the excitement

As you grow into the adult
Their love does not change
It just goes forever
And it never ends

Fathers

They are there to conceive you
They are there for the birth
Their love is overwhelming
But is not shown

Fathers fill the discipline role
Even though their love is deep
It does not surface
As often as it should

They guide you as best they can
They give you the helping hand
They are strong and emotionless
At least that is what they want you to think

Deep down inside
The feels are in abundance
Overwhelming and waiting
To be expressed

The feelings of excitement
Happiness and joy
Hurt and sadness
But most of all love

The love they have had for you
Since the first time they held you
Looking into your eyes
And touching your small hand

Fathers have feelings to
Just not seen as often
As they should be
But they are present

They need to let their feelings be known
To that child, wife and friend
It will not change how they are loved
In the eyes of others

My Daughter

You are my daughter through and through
As everyone tells me, gave me the due
You try too hard to please me and make me proud
Because I will always be proud, no matter what

You seem to struggle with decisions you make
No matter what could be at stake
You need to be a kid as long as you can
Because you will get older soon enough

Be happy and let yourself go
Don't let things worry you and keep in tow
Make sure you think things through
Because you have a good head on your shoulders

Don't let peer pressure pull you down
Because all it will do is make you frown
You need to live life to the fullest
And always try your best - for no one but you

My Son

You are the apple of my eye
And at times you make me cry
You can be anything you want to be
All you have to do is try your best

You seem to struggle in school
Even though the kids think you are cool
The sports make up for where you lack
But you can do what you set your mind to

Keep a clear head as you become a teen
No matter what your peers say, keep clean
I know you have a good head on your shoulders
And you will think before you act

I have given you guidance I know
In hoping that you will use it as you go
Making decisions through your life
And using what you've been taught to help

Always remember as you grow older
You will become bolder and stronger
But no matter what you do
I will always love you

No Matter What – They Are Loved

They are so tiny
They are so dependant
They need to be held
They need to be loved

Tiny, tiny cries
Giggle, giggle, giggle
The smile on their face
Lights up your day

Crawling to walking to running
Time begins to fly by
Baby to toddler to teens
You wonder how they grow so quickly

But even though times can be trying
You know one thing for sure
And that is no matter what
They will always be loved with all your heart

It's already been a year
And we have dried every tear
Because of the hurt we feel
As missing you is so real

You are always with us, we know
Because every day our love will flow
In the memories we all have of you
As they are kept in our hearts alive and true

The day we put you to rest
Since then has really been the test
To see how many "Mom" moments there are
As those times when you seem so far

We know you are always near
You make that very clear
We love and miss you every day
But your time had come and you couldn't stay

Mom's Life

Your life began February 3, 1941
You were married July 8, 1961
First born was May 5, 1962
Second born was April 13, 1964
Third born was June 14, 1967
Then there are your 8 precious grandchildren
All important happenings in your life

Then your life made a turn
And you needed to continue your journey elsewhere
This journey started on April 19, 2007
The night you needed to leave

We all had our "Special Tyme" with you
"Tyme" we will always cherish and never forget
As we will never forget you
The "Special Mom/Nana" that you were
You will always be missed
But you are close to our hearts.

Cards of Life

Life deals us many hands
Business, personal or just general
How we play those hands
Depends on what happens

We may play one card at a time
Or many may be played at once
Once we play those cards
It is hard to get them back

We may discard too quickly
Or hang on too long
Whatever it is that we decide
Usually affects the road of the future

Each card illustrates something different
Which means that each hand
Can be played differently
Good or bad we have to take what comes

Feeling Defeated

Life is like a bottle
You are full of giving and trying
Then you get to a point of emptiness
You feel drained and squeezed
Like there is no life left
The feeling of defeat

****

As I sit and think of you
A tear falls down my cheek
I know you are hurting
Because of love

I think of how you must feel
Losing someone you love
After so many years
Of being together

Even though I have only known you a short time
I know how I feel about you
The love that you have felt in the past
Is how I am feeling now for you

My life can be considered very serious
But I also like to have fun
Whether it be dancing naked in the sun
Or just being on a continuous run

My life gets very, very busy
But I don't know any other way
To actually sit and stay
Would make me come to pieces and fray

This would not be me
It seems that I need to be on the go
And always without a beau
But that's Ok 'cause I don't need anyone in tow

Although at times it can be lonely
Being without anyone
But I always remember to have fun
Even if it's dancing naked in the sun

****

True Love

Do you ever wonder
What is meant by "True Love"
You put 100% into love
Just to find out the other is not

One would hope to receive the same
But as time reveals, it's eery head
It is conceivably not
The way you had thought

Life can be lonely
Without someone special
Along time can be good
But also can be empty

Everyone wishes to find someone
To spend their life with
To share laughter
To share tears

To share intimate times
To be there when needed
Or to have a giving heart
When required

Love seems to come in various ways
The caring that can be shown
Toward that person in need
Or just to be there

To find someone
With the same wants and needs
Can be a life long adventure
Or it's staring you in the eye

No Answers As Yet

He sits with a drink in hand
Bottle on the table
Half full or half empty
But no answers as yet

Another drink goes down
Another glass to fill
Emptying the bottle
But no answers as yet

Pain starts to disappear
As least for the moment
Another bottle yet to empty
But no answers as yet

Bottles empty on the table
Glass empty beside the chair
Pain and ice both melting away
And yet the answers are not at the bottom

My heart is hurting, oh, so much
Even at your touch
My heart is broken in two
Because I feel so blue

I poured my heart out to you
Because we were so new
I thought you felt the same
But I am to blame

You have some issues from your past
That I hoped would not last
You need your time to sort things out
And I will be waiting once you do

I sit and wonder why
I give it such a try
Put everything I had
Into a relationship

I cared so very much
I loved his touch
The connection was strong
And I don't know why

I can't seem to get him out of my mind
Even though he wasn't always kind
I think he needs someone
More than he knows

I want to be the person he needs
To help him with all his deeds
Even if its as a friend
I want to be there for him

****

I sit and watch the clouds float by
As I, again, give love a try
When you meet someone new
You hope things will be true

As times goes along
You don't expect to much to go wrong
Then things are not what you think
And love can really stink

The "Cabin"

The "Cabin", the "Cabin" we shall go
Hoping that it will snow
Up and down the toboggan hill
While our parents are inside getting their fill

Laughter is what we hear
Because winter fun is so near
Thanks to Coop and Tuck
Because we consider ourselves in such luck

To have such a wonderful place
For us to go and be ourselves
To just be kids so we can run and play
No matter what time of day

The hill is ready all the time
Either snow or mud it is ready to climb
The wood stove is stoked inside
As we get ready for our ride

Out on the hill – staring at the top
And ending at the bottom – hoping for a stop
Grabbing the sled and back up the hill we go
Always in hope for more snow

At the end of the night when it starts to freeze
And the wind gets up to a chilling breeze
We decide to end our fun
Because we see the moon and there is no more sun

In the "Cabin" we go to warm up
And have some hot chocolate in a cup
Sitting around the fire and starting to plan
Our next adventure with the Haskett-Cooper Clan

Time To Think

Sitting at the cabin
Keeping warm by the fire
Watching the kids toboggan
Using the time to think

Reviewing the year's happenings
Trying to make future dreams
Wondering what 2005 will hold
Business, personal or just life in general

Wildlife comes and goes
Within the mystery of the bush
Sun shining on the ice covered trees
Winter wonderland at its best

****

Sitting and watching the movement of the lake
Knowing that there is always a life to take
The light rays shining down from the heaven's above
Watching the sun twinkle on the waters below

Smooth soaring hawks in the sky
You sit and ask yourself why –
Are the cards that are dealt to me
Always difficult and not made easy

Decisions as life continues
Seem to be unfair to someone
You think that life doesn't have to be this way
But things do not go as smooth as can be

It's Never Too Late to Say "I Love You"

Sitting on the beside
Of my dying Mother
Looking into her eyes
And seeing nothing

Remembering the joys
Of growing up
Pushing out the memories
Of the bad times

Waiting for the right moment
To say the words
That have not been said
For a long time

To tell my Mom
How much she will be missed
And telling her
How much she is loved

****

I sat and listened to my Aunt
Learning more and more
About my Dad
That I did not know

He had shown his mother
Caring and loving ways
As she drifted off
Into the lands of heaven

Grieving is part of life
That takes place after death
You do not realize how much
Until it happens to you

Meek and mild you wonder
'Cause he seems soft spoken
Yet he towers above
So you wonder who he really is

Does he have someone, I ask
This seems to be quite a task
To find out if he shares himself
With another person or not

He is much younger, you see
Not a chance I would have
But I would like to know
If we could get the juices to flow

Those eyes, those eyes
They make me melt
They send chills up my spine
Oh, wouldn't it be nice to make him mine

Older I am, than he
Not a chance in hell
That I might be able to tell
Someone how I feel

****

Those eyes, they sparkle
They say so much
But how to get to know
The man behind the eyes

Big, strong hands you see
Eyes of caring you hope
A quiet voice when he speaks
But you know he is too young

Looking out across the bay
Watching the water move
Into the greatest silence
And wondering what is in store

The future is always ahead
But you don't know where it leads
Or where you will be
As the year progresses

****

As I sit and watch the water
Ripple at the pier
I can feel in my eye – a tear
With this tear – there is a past

A past with a bumpy road
Wondering what is in store
If there is really anymore
For one to give and receive

What My Parents Gave To Me

As the sun hits the water
It glistens with laughter
This is what my parents gave to me
How To Laugh

As the snow floats to the ground
It can melt as quick as it falls
This is what my parents gave to me
How To Change

As the leaves change colour
And fall to the ground
This is what my parents gave to me
How To Believe

As the water slowly trickles down
The glass of the window in thought
This is what my parents gave to me
How To Think

As I go through life
I thought I knew all, but realized
I didn't because I rely upon
What my parents gave to me

Laughter, Change, Beliefs and Thinking
And to be just me

Friends Are Like The Seasons

Friends are like the seasons
They seem to come and go
But there are some friends
Who stay around, no matter what the weather

They support you when making decisions
Give you input whether bad or good
Lend an ear when needed
And just listen

These friends are people
Your learn to rely on
Even if you figure
You can handle everything yourself

You usually find out, you can't
And you need these friends
To help you get through tough times
Which can be hard to admit

Because you figure you can handle anything
No matter what is dealt
And you find you're not as strong
As you thought you were

Friends are what you make of them
You are there for them
As they are for you
'Cause you never know when you will need them

I, Thank You, for being my friend
I can always count on you
You listen and voice your opinion
Even if I don't want to hear it

You're what a true friend is made of
I just want you to know
How much I value your friendship
Every day as we go

Being There

As a little girl you look so big
As I grew, you didn't appear to be so
You were always so stern, when needed
Which wasn't often from what I remember

When I was small
I took little steps to keep up
Now that I am older
I don't need as many

You have been there for me
More often than I can count
As it seems that I back step
A little more often than forward steps

I have grown in a lot of ways
And became my own person
What I attribute to you
For making me as strong as I am

If it wasn't for your tough love
I wouldn't be where I am today
For that, I Thank You
Because I know I can move forward

The future that lies ahead is unknown
But with the perseverance you have instilled
Will help me through this time
To make my future a lot easier climb

Listen to the water crossing the sand
Hitting the shore
At a dull roar
With the help of God's hand

In comes the water at my feet
Sending a chill
But keeping me still
And with God's hand – we will meet

The cool water is touching me
It seems wet
But I do not fret
Because I know God will set me free

****

Brenda Cooper

Day In May

On a bright spring day
The birds are singing
And there is a gentle breeze
The month is May

Flutter, flutter the butterfly flew
With its bright colours
Brilliant in the sun
But not too fast for the eye to see

Brother Tom

I know we fought when we were young
Because we both had quite a tongue
It did us no good
But we thought we were the "engine that could"

There seem to be no give and take
No matter what was at stake
We would fight and fight
No matter who was right

We made mom go out of her mind
Because we were not very kind
Even though it got us no where
We didn't seem to care

We grew and went our separate ways
And there is one thing I have to say
I hope your future is what you sought
Because you can implement what you've been taught

Brother John

When I was smaller
You were always taller
Then we got older
And you got bolder

Growing up with you was a challenge
Because I felt I was in your shadow
Whether that be good or bad
It has helped me throughout life

You are quite a business man
And I will always be a fan
Because there is a lot to learn from you
All's I need is a clue

You may not have agreed with some of my decisions
That I have made throughout life
But I believe one should not prejudge
Until all the facts are given

You have quite a happy family life
And a devoted and loving wife
I hope your future gives you all the best
And your life not be put to the test

One goes through life trying to learn
Even though your parents are stern
They love you a lot, even though it doesn't always show
And you begin to wonder – Are they friend or foe

Parents have hard decisions to make
And it's not always a piece of cake
They try to guide you along the right trail
So that you can be strong not frail

You put them through their paces
With showing your parents all your different faces
Even though you get off track and out of line
They will always call you "mine"

Until you have children of your own
You will not understand the child's tone
That drives you around the bend
But always keeping in mind, your child is here to mend

Life As A Child

When you are small
Nothing seems to matter
You have no fear
But you do have a tear

Bothers and sisters you may have
To fight with and love
There comes a time
When you would trade them for a dime

As you grow older and wiser
And learn what life is about
You value your family ties
Before you say our good-byes

Now an adult you are
And you've learnt many lessons
One important one to be
Is your family tree

Sitting here alone
Wondering what life will being
Will it be rags or riches
Or queen of the bitches

Days go by quickly
Whether we want them to or not
We lose track of time
And can't even stop it on a dime

Weeks come and go
Years go by and disappear
We should stop and listen
To see what we are missing

Life is too short
To be angry and hold grudges
We need family to have and hold
And not have the family ties unfold

To My Parents With Love

Life seems to be an uphill battle
That one cannot overcome
It's nice to know you have support
When you feel like you're overrun

Your input is greatly appreciated
Even thought it may hurt
The truth can seem to be unclear
Because of emotion and a tear

Tough love as they say it is hard
But I know you mean well
Even if my feelings are low
There is still much love to flow

I, Thank You, both very much
For the love and support you gave
To help me along
And to always be brave

****

Blue Life

You think life is grand
Until something goes wrong
You try to make it right
And all it turns into is a fight

Then life just goes along
Until your happiness is gone
And life begins not to matter
While everything is a tatter

You wonder if things will change
As you begin to lose hope
On what really matters to you
Because you're always blue

Listen to the wind blowing in the trees
Passing through each and every branch
It brings music for everyone to please
As we all gather back on the ranch

The end of the day is near
And today's hard work is done
The evening appears to be clear
It is now time to have fun

The food is to the best of taste
As we finish our big meal
And sit back to see, what we're faced
When tomorrow sets in to be real

The sun is now setting
As we pull the shades to cover the light
To start our night of betting
And our minds get bright

With cards in our hands
And our mind in thinking
We each take our stand
Before anyone is blinking

The night comes to an end
Off to bed we go
Our "goodnights" we send
And we listen to the wind blow

Height

When I was small
I wanted to be tall
To be big like dad
Even just a tad

I eventually grew
To four foot two
It still wasn't tall enough
So I go rough

I grew like a bad weed
I sure did indeed
Now I'm five foot eight
And I guess my height was fate

****

Small To Tall

When you are small
And want to be tall
Your parents say
Go out and play

You want to grow bigger
So you can go figure
Why your parents say no
When you're filled with joy from head to toe

Once you have grown
And your parents' top has blown
Because you think you're in the know
And they just don't get the flow

An adult you are
You're your parent's star
And now you know why
You made your parents cry

Only To Be Appreciated

Time is like gold
And sometimes you feel undersold
Because of the time you invest
Only to be put to the test

You work as a team
Even if it's to blow off steam
Showing support and frustration
To stand behind the team of your creation

Responsibility and respect
Is what you want to detect
From your players on the ice or not
Is what should be taught

A simple "Good Job, Well Done"
Is not much to ask
For the team that you have created
Only to be appreciated

Wondering

As I sit and wait
I wonder what is my fate
What the future will bring
And if it will be a sting

Do you ever try to predict
What is in store
Down the road
And around the corner

I sometimes let my mind wonder
And I sit and ponder
Where I will be
But I guess I have to wait and see

I sometimes want to know
What the future holds
Where I will be in five years
And maybe in ten

You think you have things on track
Until you get the flack
Coming down on you without reason
And it doesn't matter the season

As you try to get ahead
No one really seems to care
You set your goals and try to achieve them
But you are knocked back for trying so hard

I Know I Need You

Even though we do not spend much time together
Always miles and miles apart
Just seeing each other on weekends
Doesn't seem to be enough

My heart hurts a lot
Especially when we're apart
Trying to detach myself from those feelings
Is when I realize I need you

Finding it hard to continue each day
Not knowing when we will see each other again
Will it be Friday, maybe Saturday
If we are lucky we get 48 hours or less

You've stolen my heart and soul
And that is why it hurts so much
Not seeing you from week to week
But there is one thing I know – I need you!

Brenda Cooper

Our Special Friendship

Since meeting you a year ago
We have a special friendship that we both know
We started out having lots of fun
Grew closer and needed to turn and run

We then had our time apart, because we knew we should
But kept in touch, because we knew we could
We have this bond that seems to flow
That keeps us together, whether friend or foe

We've had our moments, many are they
That doesn't push us apart, together we stay
You may ask why we get along
Maybe because we make each other strong

We are there for each other, not matter what
Doesn't matter if we are in a rut
We listen to what the other has to say
And no matter what the truth, we do not fray

This Special Friendship will be there along time
And the feeling we have – they will climb
But for now we have what we seem to need
And that is the friendship, that neither one of us will bleed

The Friend I Have In You

You have taught me many things
From being firm with my kids – to reality checks
You have made me face many things
Whether I wanted to or not

Since I have met you, almost a year ago
It feels like I have known you forever
There is a special connection
That will always be there

Maybe the connection will strengthen
And grow into something we will always share
Like the seventy year old couple
Walking hand in hand along the pier

But whatever happens down the road
I will always know one thing
I will always be there for you
And you will be there for me in return

The feelings I have for you
I believe you have them too
That's what makes our special bond
So strong and that's why I have "The Friend I Have In You"

My Life

Born into the world
Kicking and screaming
Not knowing a thing
But always learning

Growing up with two great parents
Trying to guide you along
Doing their best to help when needed
But not interfering

Giving advice and a helping hand
But not telling you what to do
Reaching the teenage years
And driving parents crazy, but not too often

Often enough, to make them question
Off to college or university
On you own and wondering about life
Have you made the right choices

School now finished
Entering into the work world
Changing careers throughout the years
And wondering if choices are right

Married life and children on their way
Balancing career, home life and life in general
Eight years later on your own again
Struggling with life choices, but not regrets

Children now growing and voices of their own
Need to be heard but yet too young
Marriage again but not thought about much
Balancing career, new life, children and relationship

Seven years go by – regret builds
Taken advantage of and thinking is unclear
Unhappiness settles in and does not leave
Life changes are on their way

On own again with children by side
Happiness sets in and life continues
Concentration on children and career
Life going well

Children growing and need their space
Change in location and direction of life
Relationship in future
But moves too quickly

Feelings hurt and seen irrepairable
Personal wall begins to build
Concentration back on career and children
But strong friendship remains

New relationship in the making
Friend, lover and keeper
Miles between each other weekly
But love and trust grow stronger

Feelings deepen each and every day
Talk every day – just for minutes
Future is building quickly but comfortably
Heart opens fully to include all involved

Children double in numbers
Everyone seems accepting
Balance starts to form
Love, children, career – life is fulfilled

The Love Of My Life

My love for you deepens each and every day
Because I know that you are here to stay
This distance we have between us is just miles
Because our hearts have joined as one

You are so trusting and gentle in your touch
And I can see that you care so very much
The look in your eyes gives it away
The look of love that melts my heart

I get so scared of the way I feel
My heart aches for you because my feelings are so real
I miss your hugs when you are away
But I know that you will return

Life is what we make it and no more
Even though we think we know what is in store
We think things are set out for us
Until it changes and the road makes turns

There is one thing I know and that is for sure
I want you in my life until death do us part
The good and the bad I want to be there for you
And I know that I will always be true

I have found my soul mate in you
You have captured my heart and soul
Which I never thought anyone would do
I know I have found the man I want to spend
The rest of my life with in you

Christmas Time

Christmas time is family time
It should be spent together
Laughing, crying or just talking
It is the time for sharing

The hustle and bustle of December
Remembering the real meaning of Christmas
Should bring families closer
And the past should be forgotten

Memories and more memories
Can be shared from year to year
But the time that is spent together
Should always be cherished

****

Needing No One

I am alone and always will be
I can do this all by myself
I need no one to be there for me
I can be there for everyone else

I can handle my problems and everyone else's
I am drained but I have to be there
For everyone else who needs me
Not for myself – I need no one

Life Is Like A Balloon

The air in a balloon is like a build up of excitement
The escape of air in a balloon is like a let down
Inflate, deflate goes the balloon
Just like life

The balloon gets bigger and bigger
As positive moments in life
Then you let go of the balloon
Which flies all over as air dissipates
Just as moments in life letting you down

You pick up the balloon and try again
As you put air back into the balloon
You hear a shhhhhhh sound
Little bits of air escaping

As life can be
Little let downs, one after another
Again you try and save the balloon
Plugging the hole and hoping the air will remain

As you are increasing the size of the balloon
You wince at the thought of the air escaping
The balloon keeps getter bigger
Then "BANG", the balloon bursts
Just as life can fall apart

The blue lake meets the horizon line
Like relationships in life
You think it is a straight line
But then there is a bump in the horizon

Kind of like the ripple on the lake
Can be rough, can be calm
Always remember, sooner or later
The horizon does meet the lake

****

I sit and watch the water ripple
Just as life seems to do the same
Never a smooth glass like the lake
Rough and calm, rough and calm

As life can be, never smooth
Blue as the sky can be
But can turn grey as quick as a storm
Waters can be rough as life

But as you look out over the blue lake
You remember, life is what you make it
Not what you want it to be
So you know you can handle whatever comes along

The water ripples over the stones
As life changes with time
You figure you know your destiny
But do you really

****

The clouds float through the sky
As freely as the breeze
You figure you know your feelings
Until change comes along

****

The weeks seem to long as time passes
You on the road and me at home
Knowing that this has to be
The way things are for now

I miss your touch
I miss your kiss
I miss the way you look at me
But always knowing you will return

The weekends I cherish
And look forward too
Sharing the time that we can
Pack into these short days

The time we spend together
Is very special to me
You have taken my heart
Which was not easy

I have given myself to you
In great depth
Because I know I can trust you
With my feelings

I love you with all my heart
And I know that I want you
Involved in my life
As I do not want to be alone

As a tear rolls down my cheek
I tell myself – I can handle anything
Doesn't matter what it is
Business, personal or otherwise

I pull myself together
As I remind myself – you can handle anything
Doesn't matter how much it may hurt
Or how much time it may take

I have been given the shoulders
That are broad enough to hold
Everyone's burdens and sorrows
As well as my own – if there is room

I need to be there for whoever is needy
I want to be the best I can be
Whether that be a friend or business person
I have to be the best I can be

Always With Me

I think I have my life figured out
Then all of a sudden along you come
An acquaintance, a friend but not thinking more
We start our relationship and find out there is

I take these steps very carefully
Because I do not want to be hurt again
You offer time and patience
Which I greatly appreciate

I figure I will let my feeling guide me
But I find that they move quickly
I am deeply in love with you
And after such a short time

Life is too short not to follow these feelings
I have been hesitating and holding back
But I am ready to move forward
And follow the true way I feel

Even though you are miles away
I can feel your touch – as I lay in bed
As I fall asleep with you on my mind
And I awake the same

You are such a gentleman
You have such a gentle touch
That I cherish whole heartedly
I miss you, I love you and I know you are always with me

Life - Like A Flower

Life is like a flower
The seed is planted
It grows within the womb
It's head peers out like a blossom

The flower grows and grows
Like life with opportunity
The petal spread
Like children with their wings

Then the time comes
And the petals start to fall
As our health starts to fail
Before we know it – life ends

Back to the earth
The petals go
As does our bodies
As we call it – A New Beginning

My love for you will never die
It grows more each and every day
Even though I do not make life easy
And make you question my ways
I still know I have met my soul mate
And married my best friend

****

Your dreams are your dreams
And follow them always
But take the baby steps
To follow them... then
Make them into memories

****

Dreams are what our lives are made of
Goals are what we achieve
Set your mind in a positive motion
And continue with the follow through
Like you know you can

Determination
Readiness
Effort
Attitude
Make It Happen
Stubborness

****

Time goes on and the memories of you never fade
They continue to fill the emptiness that is felt
Each and every day because you are missed
We all keep you near and dear in our hearts
As you keep a watch from above
Reminding us in that special way
That you are always with us
And will always be

****

The water sparkles in the bay
As the sun shines its ray
It is so bright, it blinds the eye
As a tear falls down your cheek to cry

As a cloud casts over the sun
Just to put a damper on any fun
One may be having on this sunny day
In the month of June not May

I guess it's about time in life for me to let go
To let go of all my love I have given you over the years
I have exhausted all avenues to try to build on what we had
The relationship that has crumbled and is no more

My love for you has never stopped
From the day I gave birth, until this day and forward
Your feelings have diminished over the past few years
And I have learn to accept that, even though it has broken my heart

But I'm sure through the years, I have broken yours
And for that I am sorry, I thought time would heal
But I was totally wrong, time will never heal
And I have now lost a child that will never return to me

Although the choice has been yours and not mine
I wish you all the best, as you make other changes in your life
May someday you find it in your heart to forgive me
For the grief I have caused you

****

Why

Do you ever ask yourself why
Why is life's road going the way it does
Why is love not what you expect
Why do children hurt one another

Why do people say the things they do
Why does love hurt
Why do people have to die
Just ask yourself why

Life Is .... Not What You Expect

Life is not what you expect it to be
You, as a child, dream of growing up
Getting married and staying with that person forever
But then life is not what you expect

You dream of having children
And being involved in their lives as they grow
Then the day comes when lives separate
And life is not what you expect

Everyone grows and matures
Starts to lead their own lives
And the ties that once were, are no longer
Because life is not what you expect

Then you think love has been found again
New beginning's at life
With someone special
But again, life is not what you expect

Some day you think happiness will avail
It appears everyone else has this
You try to change and accept
But life is not what you expect

****

As the humming bird hovers around the bright coloured flower
Your memories hover in my mind
The good times outweighing the bad
The countless hours you had me as a child, teen and adult

Your were always there for me
Giving your guidance and love
As I continue through the road of life
Your love you gave me sits within my heart

Your love will always remain with me
Along with the memories you gave me
I say "Thank You Mom" for everything you had done
As you will always remain in my heart forever

My Mom

When I was young and naive
I tended to believe
That life was unfair
Especially when I took the dare.

As my teen years approached
And My Mom as my coach
My life's experiences were limitless
I have to confess.

Entering into adulthood
And doing everything I could
To make My Mom stand up tall
And be proud of who I am.

Now with children of my own
I can really understand the tone
That My Mom had to use
When she had a short fuse.

My Mom is the greatest that can be
And I'm glad my kids get to see
What a wonderful Nana they've got
To kiss and hug them a lot.

Just Like My Dad

While I was growing up
I always looked up to one person
And I want to be –
Just Like My Dad

As years have past
And reality sets in
I have started to realize that I cannot be
Just Like My Dad

I am my own person
Who has made my own choices
Although he and I don't always agree
I'd still like to be Just Like My Dad

Accomplishment after accomplishment he has achieved
Trying to achieve my own accomplishments
I have been told time and time again
You are Just Like Your Dad

As time goes on, I know that
I will never be Just Like My Dad
But I will remember on thing
He will always be My Dad

As the wind blows through the seasons
Memories of you are always with us
Whether we are at work or play
Your memory is with us to stay

It is 2 years on April 19th
When we had to say our final good-byes
As you needed to continue your journey elsewhere
In a place with no pain

You are missed each and every day
But you will always remain in our hearts
As your presence is always felt
And we cherish the love that you gave us

Four Years Ago
The Angels Came From Above
To Take You Away
Even Though We Wanted You To Stay

We Knew That The Time Had Come
When We Had To Say "Goodbye"
As Hard As It Was To Let Go
We All Knew It Had To Be Done

The "Goodbyes" That We Said
Are Just "Hellos" In Waiting
As We Will See You Again
But In A Different Way Of Life

Life continues even though you think it might not;

Because you are missed each and every day;

It has been 3 years since you continued your journey elsewhere;

There is not a day that passes where you are not thought of;

Your laugh can be heard at a distance but

your presence is always close;

Your absence is felt each and every day;

But your memories are always with us in our minds and our hearts.

****

A MOTHER

A mother is someone that is always there
Someone to talk to
Someone to cry with
Someone to laugh with
And someone to love

A mother gives unconditional love
No matter what you do
She is there with her arms out wide
Ready to give you a hug
Or a kiss if needed

A mother is not always appreciated
For all she does for everyone

Edwards Brothers Malloy
Oxnard, CA USA
January 23, 2015